Mulholland Dive
Copyright © 2025 by Vanessa Roveto
Cover & Interior by Joel Amat Güell
ISBN 9781960988553

CLASH Books
Troy, NY
clashbooks.com
Distributed by Consortium.
All rights reserved.

First Edition: 2025
Printed in the United States of America.

POETRY

 @clashbooks    @clashbooks    /clashbooks

Email: clashmediabooks@gmail.com

MULHOLLAND DIVE

VANESSA ROVETO

"I read this hypnotic poetry book in one sitting. At first, it hurt my feelings because I thought the narcissistic love interest was me. Then I realized it's poetry and abstract and the character was many people and things. Or maybe it was all me and none of it was me, and either way it didn't matter because the best books should hurt the writer's lover's feelings. So I wiped my tears and finished the book and realized it was absolutely perfect in every way, much like Vanessa Roveto herself."

—Anna Dorn, author of *Perfume & Pain*

"Vanessa Roveto's *Mulholland Dive* is the newest entry into louche, brash, riveting Los Angeles poetry. '...a shopping list is a suicide note i'm performing.' Car crashes, smut, lesbian pillow talk...this isn't your grandma's poetry, but if it was, the world would be a better place. I am really impressed by this book."

—Ben Fama, author of *If I Close My Eyes*

"This is the singular kind of book that calls to me. *Mulholland Dive* is a thing of strange beauty, jagged, mournful, orgasmic, sonically exhilarating. Vanessa Roveto uses language like Francis Bacon, grinding it until image and emotion are, in her words, meat-soft. Each fragment touches on the chaos of death and self and desire in 21st century Los Angeles, in such a precise, visceral, original way, it makes Lacan's objet petit a textually attainable."

—Alistair McCartney, author of *The Disintegrations*

"Every line in *Mulholland Dive* sings a perfect note. A prismatic ode to the enduring enigmatic concept of Hollywood as a container for death and blondes, of lesbian heartbreak, of motherless and fatherless girls, of the human struggle to survive; Roveto has created a crucial work of art that contributes to our understanding of beauty as form, of womanhood, of what it means to love and hurt and be hurt."

—Elle Nash, author of *Deliver Me*

it was the year us girls had a feminine desire to go missing

MULHOLLAND (DADDY'S DEATH) DRIVE

meanwhile the cars still swerved off Mulholland Drive. I'd gotten off the plane in the Dream Factory, in tropical berlin, then followed a beautiful woman around the last months of a highway turning my curved extravaganza. upon impact wet jewels detailed my rescue. back then it seemed as though I needed to feed on my own skin, cutting into my own ability to feel again. I felt so much I needed so much more than holes. a diva low-definition video playing hollywood starlet embracing. I'm here for the We dream when I woke up I started the slow climb toward i, opening the car crash to lose possession: isolated from a paramedic i mean a pandemic's whisper. my relation to the fetish of the perfect actress's apartment: hugely infantile. this bifurcated dialogue is a lesbian form of lame pillow talk. lines conjugate the swish. the film frames margins maims my small-town tune. a cubist portrait in the mirror tells me to come back home and get married as the room's twilight makes use of desperation. instead i become a blonde and answer the phone's casting call for smut. girding this cursed project, the ancient root of a palmtree, a form of seeing that will be unrecognizable until it's not. someone's done this before, says it's been real. a lip injection stiffens the details

at the gay bar somehow everyone knew the actress was
into bestiality. encounters with the ever-elusive Real.
i found out the easy way and yet: some investigations
kick off and never return. so she rents herself to a
complex with a shallow pool gone empty, nightmarish
haunted house. *what's she looking for?* hey there, Fantasy:
a starring role as the tomb of an unknown actress,
southern California, 1940s, voluminous tits, balloon
pricks. the dead manager is someone who calls the
cops on forgetfulness. it's a question of the angle i told
myself and began my research into hallucinations. this
research looked like sifting violence on the sand, feeling
the punch of rapping girls, smashing pills without
marrying them. i became estranged to the lawn hairs
surrounding me begging for a stiff cocktail. i even
begged to the someone who was stationed there by my
own brain

on my first day i notice the world bears my beauty mark.
my nose structures the landscape. what is not platinum
blonde becomes progressively obscured becomes a soft-
hearted body for frosted ghosts. their lackluster hair
without shine, a brutal coat. the untimely returns but
never gets erect. in the same way an awareness is built
about one's late-coming artistic process at age 43—you
try clawing at your own cunt, you try weaving astroturf

here an eruption of heat is the most silent part of the day: my online profile a story of a possible homicide, a closetful of a (fashion) victim's clothing

when i became Rita my fingers burned red flares: i bought 17 varieties of silk wigs. they rubbed shoulders while i went searching for our dialogue. i developed a tension for low-hanging orbs, abalone smiles, switchblading

often with a name no one knows what's being referred to. I's are costume options, they admire the fey

She (my director) says *hey there pretty girl it's time to wake up*

i'm lost in the quarantine: what to do with my wreckage?
before the head accident i only remember riding around
with daddy as the waning sunset degraded into need.
the pearlescence of clutched beads breaking ground
toward the Corpse of Discovery. a masque used to
clean the house held in abeyance

      isolation of cheap clothing tatters
      the color of fake bruises/pretty waitress veins
      I didn't fit in much anywhere

later decades, Later: in Beverly Hills i remember that
her him died a sweet passing. after which Age came to
combine dessert with poppers stretching tight black
jeans across a loose colon. Her mourned herself

in this slap of death the 70s fridge cracked itself open as
the words broke unobstructed onto tile. Age was called
on to repair and de-thaw the soul. but the heartbroken
celebrity vase staggered, forgot the murmur, scarred the
gush ball

outside the pool's deflated raft a housewife's torn voice
is undressed and dragged across

domestic spatial geometries: some things immediately
towel off the condensation

How worn did she look the onlookers went outloud

confined to the Valley, a snake began to live in this mistress's pores: crawling out of her alleys only to tongue-touch. often the townsfolk carried her corpse after she slumbered on the cold slab for too long. crazy self-punishment was our guidebook to a miniature hard-on. sometimes "She" was posed as a rat, the same scavenger that stood there one century ago, the streams ferrying their cargo the same streams as two months ago, their bushes fellowed and planted and tendered. ongoing lip loss pressed release and cast out as a wanderer, an exiled head wound: from man from woman from the serial killing

at the movie's set her drug discovers a goddess in a
Cadillac, slicked feathers across leather, flapping angels
providing abuse and anorexia. the child actress pulls a
smiling face out of her back pocket and blows it over a
castle, over a gagging princess dining on tiny scabs

there are no fathers in this film. the putrid sins the
sacrifice the atonement that could only be cured by rest
and relaxation. i have no friends. i am the star

a billboard above Echo Park Lake says: *We're all frictionless post-dildo.* so i decide to blind date and grope the sun subbed to her hair: seems someone's blonde is my new girlfriend. the cell's phone tells us to light a candle for all the departed souls paddling for their lives on giant swanboats. they were thrilled by the sound of their name buried in feathers. the air sieved lungs, smogthickened. the light-hair shows me a piece of bruise on her lips and i look in the pond to drown the weirdness. the sexual chemistry of a psycho floated across the damp surface. witch jetstreams: mysticism was the distance needed from

in the crimson desert she was all these characters:
everything that happens to Giuliana is Giuliana. a
traumatized Italian is sometimes served up in the fifties
sometimes right now. *how long is a 6 month relationship?*
said the subtitle who quickly disappeared behind the
curtain

i realized advice can be really easy or really hard.
this milestone was an engraved key, like everyone's
appearances living rent-free. while watching the
reflection i remember my mom said all hysterical
animals are eventually taxidermied

in the real-like hospital a sequence invented the kabuki of caring, the traumatist personae. coats opening and closing to show. this is where scary lives says nametags giving consistency to the lifeline pleading for perspective. meanwhile Dad's weight was written in kilometers on a dry-erase board while the sheets tangled his years in threads. he thought he was Brian Wilson, sand beneath his toes, pet sounds. negation doubling indemnity. in emotional terror management it's either half-past midnight or half-past

the fragments of time followed eyes shaking out of getwell cards sent from last year. no mail could contain these monsters in wait. love hallucinates/love dads the half-past man did not meet her eyes. the wires hanged themselves from the ceiling, fearing the end of masculine. together we all played chest support and left it up to the other ghouls to fill our oatmeal trays. at night we punched all the buttons watching for someone, wanting someone to come so badly. curtains were married before the toleration and the letters flowed from the yoke on his back. the harsh lights yelled for codeine cocaine coma whatever. normalcy requires a camera crew. the TV subtitled a housewife speaking english, killing the vibe when the hospital delirium started dad was in new york looking at a Modigliani show from 1989. today he was on the 5th floor becoming garden, one cutting after another

they wouldn't let him leave because he couldn't. his life felt left

and i his childless daughter playing actress, was soggy, bloated, hungover, and wanton. i was the barren plant god refused in me, it wouldn't give me a baby

says my mother whose id is dying. that fake sunflower in your lap is a psy-op says the nurse

Lana del Rey's chemtrailing over the sky outside
your hospital window outside your life. this was cold
comfort, like the beepbeep machine is all i can hear in
my ear all this year i mean this daytime is a conduction
you're consuming it on your time tell me what to do.
a curious transfer growing into a quiet connection via
redpills touch under a bodiless pandemic. teenagers say
torn jeans hide the fragile. why is adulthood so illusive

my cancer is sun and

you're floored in the United Church of God's Monsters
pulmonary plenary axis man's hands the ceiling painted
with faded sky sotto de voce sotto di su: Capital's death
mask

they're no time left

i took time off, became a clock, as the beginnings of
spring discovered randomness. privacy walled to cover
my fears in the heartbeat monitor overlapping with
the bird's chorus inside is outside and outside march
blossoms like a lily opening its sternum unfolding to
a raw color i don't know the name of it or anything i
don't know the name of this feeling but i know that
when you went the world went nameless went still like
the monitor sitting there like the woman my mother's
sitting beside you holding that fake flower's voicebox:
reweeding the beginning of a dream

later on the way home from the hospital the car pulled
itself over for a violent crying jag

after which the Phantom calculated the hypnotized girl's losses against the suffering sum of saints, a chapped-to-blood lip, boulevards of broke. she put on his blue flannel shirt because one day she will self-handle a phillips head driving thigh-deep, start balding

i was ashamed of my ball rage, and tried to drive it out. i hurriedly purchased a fake fur coat and pink lipstick to conceal my growing throat spasms. somewhere a baby tooth began falling into the hand, an incisor of a minor accusation like a dial on a stereo turned down low: everybody's least favorite pop station playing the 90s across the underworld

the woman fed the Santa Ana winds her thinning doll
hair. the lizard's skin was lotioned up daily, moisturizing
the scales. mom told me Former Dad had arrived at the
neptune society of ashes to dust. a storm was gathering
under the sheets, dirt was on the other side of the door,
begging to be sorted and remembered. tumbleweeds
movie'd across the ceiling in a circling patterning the
frame. his omega watch begged for a new wrist to
keep time. i put a cowboy hat on top of my bandages,
allowing the tears to crawl back into their sockets

this feminine-specific grief was singular but dad was a universal concept tested against the soft lightbulb dangling bare from the motel's ceiling. this mourning a salivating american doll, a dirty word in Latin, a seeking out of random. the leather chair's arm reached for the phone to call dad about the passing of dad, him. the cable cord was entering its afterlife as the optic nerve separated into rods and curds. hairlike legs crawling out of her eyes were now called lashes. the cheap ashtray was a medium conjuring the remnants of our last karaoke party: a Madonna and child's playlist was the gist of it. the next day men's names became men's initials carving into westerning skin. dying in spring is the cruelest month this resident where mom lives is now the only place i have had to pay sweat over slumber. at the memorial sharing dad is our chapped matryoshka. my best friend avoids her husband's stained rug while my girlfriend researches dream homes for my inability. luckily my sister sleeps through time in a womanly matter. each child a stained tree ring. it became 3 in the morning and i was hoping the beer would execute me until i was 44. the dust on the floorboards became known as our dearly departed and we swept with care. the spoiled little apricot sitting in the corner a reminder of the oxygen, of the boy child. no fake lashes to hide the bipolar ghost vs badass of my face. my neighbor's head tells me that some doll's eyes shed real paint a dream in which a shopping list is a suicide note i'm performing. in it i bought sixteen varieties of ornamental weed. i rubbed the nubs on my shoulders while we were searching, running away from the name molly on a napkin including other drugs and ex-girlfriends. then a ferry was taking off in possession of his penis indicating the Nile was moving in two directions in the present. sometimes reality swims past its verdict sometimes the xtralarge world is real. i awoke to an Oscars standing ovation in my room just as the crow's feet marred my limbs i became a hoodie concept: an empty head worn around the shoulder. that night my grief was sold discounted online to the lowest bidder, one of the greatest regrets of my life. and just recently my period ran three laps alongside five red T-shirts fighting cancer. blood glucose was a compass. no chemo no more. the sad wig made its girlfriend sleep on a sheet of plywood laid across the kitchen table. the soup stain on dad's neglected t-shirt was desperately longing for throw-away mercy

this House of Intuition lost its mind and began to provide remote shamanic service. its once frisky tits clipped toward shrewd fingers burnt raw from dark chemicals

INLAND EMPIRES

i go to Elysian fields and wait for succulents to speak at me. sometimes their sad voice is in the human carvings on crumpled green, half of what it used to be. sometimes their voice is an oxygen effect moving me along the paths away from the audience breath, the blurry playground, or the elderly who are looking for their own land of enchantment, maybe a place where they are appreciated as sentience

the last six tragedies i passed are my pathway

drugged. a place is made like this

in the west my sleep begins to model a blonde's pleasure. the self consciousness of the uncanny: this dyad of the feminine and the homosexual, this hormonal treatment. the penalty for having loved is despair. *i was beautiful last year*

i never return too

disordered beyond its rise: she wore an ass so tragic she could no longer look at it. she was on the wrong side of 30, collecting water. her tits no longer conical, the patina of rebellion cracked lips. she was a lesbian of a certain age. she was a raging chocoholic, her mediocrity was rewarded. this is not an opera. sometimes people disappear

i chose my name based off a poster

because another person i love is gone: the shape is a weird zero when she climbs into bed. the wanting computer plays that McCartney song about being amazed over and over. maybe i'm amazed at that way you're not being here. maybe i'm amazed at that new great ass of yours, an organizing principle you once sold me. on the desk coagulated milk shames coffee into a ball of crumpled need. tumbleweeds of hair on a pillow leak empathy for 5 minutes of tears and sad head. later the photograph was interred i would pay anything to have Dad as a ghost haunting the gravesite of Raymond Roussel, locus soloist. the world bristled with the Hegelian horror of totality the diabolic dialectic of negation the exposed contract of conspiracy seeds of subversion seeds of dissatisfaction the saddest head the world has ever been given. in grievance culture we organize our plots according to. cement. she watched her homelessness from a place postfixed. the devil wore cheap hair extensions penetrating pockets of soft. god was cunted i ask the direction dialogue to tell me in what act this new age will cum. a performance artist signifying strangeness, this character was a dead divorcee on her way to an online male model. she was tripping on dissonance, the death drive, the masochist, not a dry eye in the house but hers. this was a strategy in no sense. trying to quit sugar, i dreamt my new name was Soufflé. that's when the human condition goes to outer space. (once again i think i live in Poland). i wanted to please her. i think i need to try. i attempt to follow a path that says okay back to Dada's road film. this is a fantasy with gloves off: a high school industrial complex. *the film is a fish eye's view of women* according to the species. i want to finger her need it's the only way my hair won't go gray. but she's a silent star. i get off on it. someone has a blue key carved to fit her slot as we walk toward Hollywood Boulevard, an area known to play a major role in the history of woman slavery, serving as the largest prostitute trading center in the country, established circa 1895. our mouth gets sore from this life sentence. the lock socket burns from wanting entered. through the windshield's vaseline'd lens we gaze femme fatales blurred details making her immediate danger all the more clear after which i stroke a metal strip and i drive thru rows of smoked grass to LA's River. it's on the downlow with a failed metrorail above and midway is an island naming its post. there was once a church there that welcomed the concept of Should and hated all that children could muster. we are the bottom of the shock, no market value. no names no faces no markers say how or why and when. frequency drowned. this median is the center of hell. trauma belongs to the body but can no longer contain it so there i went and there i go. progress flows and flowers downriver from a grief picnic. a shipwrecked survivor must have reminded us because our We wouldn't. i feel the scream the hot showers began and ate her out ate it like a zombie. Tahiti people say *you eat life or life eat you.* so i bought a razor, a vibrating butt plug, a subscription to a collection of streaming shows that i draped over myself like quilts. i named the butt plug Shelly and i was too happy not to judge myself measuring bummed tits up against the impossible perfection of suds. the soap was never strong enough. the scream took over and no dry space went unkempt as i forgot the master-market's glamor decorum, bitterly driving my teeth into gone-bad scum. my lungs filled with chlorine as i remembered a lost belly's rub the pretty strangled waitress used to serve these language artists, rubbing them without pain. kissing gender goodbye, women selling women to woman was the romance comedy, slut poetics. this book binds the masses. over there: femme mayhem, lady torture. the coming-of-middle-age the coming of women anticipating anticipation itself. over a kale salad my brother asks since dad's dead if we could share a pronoun. on the itemized bill Cum Dodger is what gets written without being spoken it was months after the film never premiered when someone 6 feet away yelled they put cum in the vaccines. i ask my mom to un-heart this meme. i'm still haunted by the straight lady who asked when lesbians know they're done with sex. oedipus would have loved all these available milfs in his area with god given insight

i hear another gay named every woman he met Whitney Houston

just like Schrodinger's Pussy where observing something could have no bearing on its state: all us homos were believed to be history's oldest recorded roommates these corpses lubricate cinema: Bonnard's vagabonding is a body-thing. anal cancer is conflated with the blonde femme mayhem of playing hardest to get. when life left your male body time entered it: an index of the temporality, every bad crime movie that drank itself to death. dead objects last forever in borderline-personality culture. this American screen's face cannot see reality, only the zoned-out, the aphasic as fuck

like the video where Kim Kardashian expresses herself from the inside producing herself from herself then reproducing. any me being free therefore whereas a name doesn't signify. so i followed the blonde to riverside. we had been in the town of Interiors for one week. in this road bar every woman was called money and the screens split them ripping. what am i doing? how do i get my body into that position on the pool table? perhaps not signifies but represents. a ghost-scape creaming reproduced reality, shiny dripdrops of bitters. my heart was punched into this desert. at the stool in the corner the goggles pushed themselves aside and began reading her diary. she was my cipher my overseer my mental warden after getting stabbed and passing away as Sue, Laura is Nikki again in this triptych time-painting of tomorrow. the other actors were in warsaw. there was a sex part and they were also killed. converting our eyes with our hands i'm in america, then i'm in a jewish hole, snowed in and sausage-made to the sounds of Strange Fruit. the film's tagline is a blonder Andy Warhol woman doppelgang-raped. on the walled surface a curling poster of a rabbit talking nonsense. does it too belong to the blurring? these latent feelings last exactly 3 hours 24 frames per. drinking the Kool-aid to oblivion provides no successor. morning comes to say *it's been real* i like things but i like this hot suburban actress more, the sex work, the funeral pyre, a hysterical crypt currency. a cubicle of air, trapped in an 80s microwave. drooling at every memory's monument, the cutoff jeans oscillated and slipped askew from the weight of mourning. the prop master's gun crumpled the shot sheet dripping beyond any poetry. my wife will kill you if she finds out you facefucked your head's director

this sounds like dialogue from our script

she played it as it plays: events came into her girlfriend's mouth. the women fantasized an entire generation's secret screaming, ennui. Maria (Wyeth's?) oral-anal fixations were responsible for the pillow's coitus rejection. the asylum-goers described her dancing as "posthuman." across the room the former man sent phonetic transmission but did not have eyes: all the sockets fearing this penile goddess. the other guests in the room tended to fill our baked bean holes. sadistic elements entered like a piece of fuzz caught inside the lip. a vacuum's brush inhaled it all propelled by circumstance this miner's cart went hurtling through her caves. one deserves no credit for sitting in it. i was an extra, no SAG card, a soft scalp depressed against the audience's delusion. this damaged supermodel shaving everything pubic away just for a gaze to the camera for warmed-up human content. anybody can crawl into an abattoir, make their movie a shabby revenge thing. a forgotten alcoholic mustache, Johnny Depp, goes straight to video i wanted this new blonde to be as happy as my first clam. an italian by birth the director asked that she was drenched in her own pasta sauce but i had misplaced the pot. in the next scene the blazer set itself aside to make way for a black thong. Lynch made her go through dead-dad's desk to show you a picture of me inducing myself into a skinny girl coma

illuminated doodles: the needle hits her arm and she's lifted into heaven by a bunch of assholes from San Diego. this is the role sex plays scratching into the place where the kitty clawed accidently, flare-ups appeared on my arm. i bought celebrity vitamins and replaced daddy day care with vegan super-ego goo. i rubbed this all over my body's outline. luckily when my dialogue said i don't know why an actress's gender is lost at midlife she said i appreciate you. at the time i was semi-posthumous i was never impregnated but my whole world changed when entering the film Arts academy to discover vampires who hadn't felt things for hundreds of years. my mentor was a lukewarm body, a mom haircut, Kate Winslet

Sue's depressed and despondent, befriends the Valley Girls. their nonexistence causes her to cry. alternately, they may actually exist, but who has the gallstone to complain about being betrayed? what business was it of hers? though it was apparent when Jeremy Irons lies heavy on her belly. their director-actress love was bolded innocent and strange. her inner-tubes made an effort to look cute when moved and tucked aside by a T-shirt into blue jeans. too bad her eggs were airborne and stale. a classic Phantom's backstory, she lost the curse. on the call sheet my uncanny Valley mother wrote *my husband died today* and no one will ever write that about me her blouse unthreaded and scalloped to free sad sapped sagging tits that bared unease. the sexless culture watching choked relief at the sight of nothing in bed 3 movie hours apart twitching shoulders. the erotica of total fucking boredom an enema an edible dance macabre

in another time zone mom said scream therapy is making a lot of you worse. it was clear the paraplegic was tired of locking eyes with the famous horse. in another version of the cowboy script the bi-curious addict was looking forward to hearing from both men women and other devils

all the while she was shuffling closer to a human coil, dreaming someone cut off my head

dad played the role of father he recently left behind

i learned ti amo in the script to study. Red Desert
Dialogue is a communist with a limitless sex
drive. mentally this Italian actress shared a bizarre
infantilism: there's Giuliana exercising her psyche
out in public again. no wonder her son is a paraplegic
and a jealous husband. no psychoanalysis or thought
structures could suture her whole. she is the pioneer of
no comment a new poetics of never forgetting her labic
pain. the plurality of *vitto* (boarding) into Vitti: she's
the embodiment of checking out early. Vitti as in *video*.
a sequence where sun splashes across the protagonist's
lashes i want to tousle them to filter reality who says
real is more. tonight on screen she tells her son she's
somebody she can't know. somebody knew someone
he didn't about the car crash before the film begins.
now she punches into a voiceover so speaking becomes
dubbed. the director wants us to know she isn't her

words mention her, Monica Vitti, an identity card built to puzzle. a performance loophole into minimizing responsibilities. her meaning breaks down into the incomprehensible as she takes language down the alimentary track in that spaghetti commercial. my dad told me she was everything out of reach, women-curving sadness. he was dead when he told me as sunshine splashed across a swimming pool's pink swan raft in the valley. deflated pleasure cocktails. unglamorized. i said te amo so many times to him as he showed me the jagged scar on his arm in unsubtitled foreign but that was another film. i'm back in the amnesia pavilion with a Justin Theroux tattoo called A Woman in Trouble. it's the day after my birthday and my new gardener, a screenwriter, cut off the branches exposing my hole to all the neighborhood dogs. i was ashamed to abandon myself to their gaze and hurriedly ran to purchase a new full bush costume. *how many seasons do girl hips last?* i needed to conceal my age spots my muscle spasms my pillow princess my wandering personhood. sunshine splashes across the veranda just missing Laura's hair, purposing sadness. a crystal vase pleads for peonies cut to bleed blush

MARIA
(COVID CRUSH)

Maria came and went with season's blooms, as the violets turned the blue the nail color's girliness covets. we were found when the world had a bad cold when mother natured. when the light fissured through the skylight kissing an animal performance. that year there wasn't a single redwood to break, there was only Maria. her youth had been bleeding all day shedding into the sweet creek seeking approval from a wealthy mistress. a roll of nickels smelled the odor

complaint was the mourning that spring. i wrote
"the" before Maria, i rode the hard gray edges of her
pandemic mouth. she didn't quite believe in the virus.
actually

she was the sort of cripple that made dating feel like
tourism. Girl Scout gravity without regrets. *does this
girl cum with the couch?* i don't no. i try not to think of
Rebecca my most recent sex toy. her rubber kiss. or
when the alarm clock disappeared under a miniskirt
while the beer bottle stretched its neck to ravish privacy

counter-transferring moments tip per tip. collapsed and
boneless. meanwhile i was a pair of canceled cushions
and Mistressed. we know things by their refuse

when she first said hello they were climbing peaks with airborne humor toward sky daddy. they populated her worlds through self-support within her pink walls she counted. blood marrow was measured through a convoluted calendaring system

the news of the event stumbled from the tv to Celine to Babygirl to the space on the ground where shame sprouts its cracks

the texture of my date's thoughts was fake fur

night began when she dreamt about me, sleeping with Laura, waking up through raw food chomping comforting gloomy June with her itchy sheepskin and self-soothing licks. in the morning she came to me like a child and said *i dreamt you liked old movies you were helping me construct Maria's tinder smiles.* Maria smiles

because daddy issues are an eternal struggle. Dad is the sun that holds us accountable, holds

illusions. lack of transition is what i felt lost most because i loved blooming i loved attracting degradation. i live for the cute. when i was a teenager i copied this image. it was of my biceps flexing to a kitty to enliven youth. a lunar eclipsing feline's touch. copying is a form blurring the reflection, lipstick-wide kisses on a Chateau Marmont napkin

a mourning dove bursts through its pollen

we met for real at the Semitropical bar, she wearing fake blonde and me this time bottled brunette. where the elegant skinned creature under her armpit was a part-time show. i was masqued. turns out Maria was unemployed as she drove her boss-pussy straight into the banquette's chapped upper lip. inside the wallpaper bled jacarandas in a reserved space where mannequins discussed how a host envelopes a new guest. i watched with an open face: question marks relaxed their wrinkles. i breathed in the ducts i endangered my fingertips against her selfish clay. my date was an Artist bloodletting older women. i was unlike the other women in her life who were never people. nor plants. mostly they were workout shorts who consorted with men who like to tell us we don't have to cover our pretty noses to avoid catching. i studied her roots. outside the crescent moon was getting bent over the next time we saw each other was dated Scorpio Season. it was trash day so the car took us on an unclean drive. this time she opened the passenger door wider and exposed her pretty socket to a billboard advertising her queercore. circling around the slots she eventually slammed into my soft pottery. i grabbed my scalpel and other loose tools to give viewer feedback. *how does the artist get her body into that position?* she was priestess i was nature morte. like Lucien Freud nudes i learned much by assing in place. across Sunset a torn pornstar looked past a time we didn't yet know existed. We stopped editing after i was parted that night my website felt insecure. the haptic feeling of a demon's exchange. Maria had screened me just like the prehistoric times when meaning was given not problematized. having said that she was driving on the wrong side of the 101. she was 30 or something she was mealy-mouthed she reignited the practice of referring to Holly Wood as Heidi Fleiss. Fleiss flying beyond poetry, her meaning not given. Heidi said *ur a prisoner if you care.* this isn't about Heidi but about Mary #2. i don't know who Mary No.1 is. doubt that's her real name though. doubt she's a virgin mary (let's call her Maria). this video wouldn't know trouble if it hit it thru the vaseline lens of mom's attachment. the open sore was syntaxed, oozed into

just before me Maria was a quarantined hangup's
nudie pic. she had caught the mean bug from a recent
boyfriend a semi-dead meat puppet named Jalfrezi.
she'd squirt onto this zombie and play stranger. the cut
had became the suture. he consumed her lonesome like
Jean Luc-Nancy's writing on community labor BDSM.
mary became nancyboy and took a hiatus from the self.
Magritte'd and transitive. a pipe that was never quite
there obfuscated by a peep showing

on Day X we took to walking the street again. our
dialogues pushing knowledge into art applying thought
into power moves. June gloomed and only a ripped-
gay pushing a lawnmower shirtless got in our way. in
the way nothing opens the way out of. we discussed
nothing. our MFA education kept its arms folded as
we watched a set of loose hair rollers tumble paving
gratitude. an abandoned pair of crutches indexed out
mutual sickness. like me i knew she had drunk in
others' wet injuries had bristled against a ghoul or two.
liberalizing juxtaposition, she too had been triptych'd

later we're beached in a Malibu hotel and she's in my hole like a promise ring. seems a bottom is also the top. her east coast broke and yoked this western. the beads of sweat on my forehead could only be explained thru a cop's contortions. a corps of discovery an erotic commodity she was a real housewife a dominatrix a wildebeest and more. her spirit ex was our third and my first menage. she preferred the scent of Dior No. 2 behind her because she already knew that hole. we mimicked coworkers. minutes flew past a pink bikini rubbing up against homemaking. no one knows how to convey subjecthood anymore (*when I was born when i died*). a walled seashell display coffins pearls pleasure. quiet hearts of darkness. above the shrine a framed image of a mollusk rendered speechless noon comes every wednesday: every day is a wednesday every day. in those years we all suffered Dead Mother syndrome. others observing life through binoculars worn backwards like the libertines in Salo, like Salome's endless parade of white doilies. i was a cutout star method out to translate souls. there is no film without mother, with a divine womb in trouble. a similar situation unfolds in Jellyneck's Piano teacher. Erika mutilates and begs for symbolic rape: these "adults" who return to body-hatred and residual cock, the worst combinations of baggage always reminiscent of the relationship between a head session and a free persona. genitals just make themselves right at home

that summer's Marine layer was a cop's rough kiss.
rioting ceremonial gestures of punching a hole into a
pot. the past alighted by impact. mom and i smoked
grass for fodder, took up gardening. this awkward
grammar boner choked out the intersections of all
the new trends all the options across plant-like plant-
life. i'm not sure when my ass became conscious of the
object market's sobbing selfie display. only language can
free us from language. like every Albee i named my new
cactus Sylvia and made it love me

like an oozing paint blob on a Francis Bacon sizzle, a character organically generates itself into text. (opposite, below) work dissociated from fact triggering an idea of the open face pope stimulated by Velasquez simulations. the unconscious desire of the brushstrokes to inflict damage, transubstantiating Christ's ventriloquists into a pig's carcass. the spine separating the golem from the flesh. hm

soon these hard corns lifted right off my toe. taxidermy had gotten in the way of pleasuring. so the lonely dad suit was salt-dried and interred that entire season we tripped. we abandoned religion and became nutjobs. at the desert spa We was slippery when wet with the occult geography of a craftsman's feng shui. we refused dichotomies but not difference. cinnamon girl played on the radio while we traveled back to california to 1970 to Zabriskie point on a tiny flying carpet under our tongues. it was purely visual our open mouths silently screaming thong implications. the rock graffiti began to fade as the sun steeled itself against the sky, refracting a girl body's backlit fragments

echoing Judd's concrete pieces that broke the desert: we tempted Death into dissociation it was mid to late summer that we began to love in-path. i changed the outdoor light bulbs to less bright, more golden. it was when we tripped to the spa, finally admitting she was an understudy in chanting, that i smiled and it made my summer truthfully

at this unvaccinated desert Maria took a sample she wanted uttered. only the 60s bathing suit advertising smooth LSD tits burst my defensive cysts replacing them with belief in the supernatural. a baby's oil slicked

as the sky staged a sundown from our private deck the tiny owl on the roof astral-projected, allowing us to forget our labial trust issues turns out the two wigs that looked alike were the same. cynicism is the Greek word for never getting laid said the blog post then shot itself in its head. the algorithm's thanatophobia kept the social distracting. i instead came to believe in the healthful effects of poison, in quilting the pink into french. eventually the lost monument no one could remember, Paris Hilton, was mourned. i still found her inner-tubes fascinating. she was my subway cop my c'est la vie baby

vice gripped her radical edict her sexual desire for the
aged. i went back to meat i went full-on Bacon. Francis
talks about the cynicism of Macbeth's tomorrows.
there's no purpose only respiration only a medium
for accident. the Occident rode away on the Thames
at high tide. the theme of the story was the present, a
heavily gessoed painting of a weird cave. the emotional
life gets in the way the painting gets in the way of

soon Nothing cums for hours. it was hard for her
breaking the willed articulation. a lunatic left chance
up to chance

i develop a habit called ketamine. it tells me death is not an intellectual exercise. the paint was dedicated to her and dictated. the gesso touched its own attributes. cruelty is incompatible with abstraction and womanhood can only bear so much reality. they're either joining the church or joining the anodyne or cultivating a preference for torment over commonplace annihilation. Bacon preferred to torment himself with these screaming hell brushstrokes to allow the chance of escaping. Mary and I had a beautiful joint cruci-fixation on the oral phase. in which the painting's background colored us into

POST-MORT

Mort was the balance between finding form in one's function and function in one form: eyes jabbing into hooks hooking the eye hole whole. an untitled diptych. a mort of total absorption was both convincing and impersonal, propaganda. amor a feeling remote a train stop a fedora on a suitcase facing the sun. and the next Polish train wasn't coming for hours

Nikki was my third negative covid text that hot vaxx summer of dazed & confused razed & buried from the indoors. she had a more "human" look than i did. first of all she was beheaded then easily resurrected. mom made a poem about this topic and also Lenin titled Happiness. so i updated my dreams. worlds elided. i notice Hilda who runs the sandwich shoppe still has a little statue of mort for sale. mortadella. the box puts its skin back on: something is there and at the same time why mix a child into war? the sculpture was a girl with flowers providing historical context. there are no more real girls left. i taught my imaginary daughter how to count using the same number of daisies. the paint remained until the monument was dismantled. the bronze statue read peace to me but

Morte had been replaced: was she an artist or an image, or just a lossy loser?

the artist caught in ions short-circuiting of monuments of movements braced for an onrush a harlequinade. the pathos the caricature of Jennifer Coolidge's lips. behind every clown is a story that transcends its artifice. i missed the meaning just. "just." no caption as Yvonne Rainer rained *dance is hard to see* so she unsaw: foregrounding concepts, opening up a cancellation. a pixelated Madonna video of a woman looking at a woman look

three see-scapes. a solo: 1) her black-cloaked tracing the peripheral 2) slow-mo(aning) to furniture 3) a gauzed fit of guttural woman-screaming drowning Rachmaninoff to center the stage. i took apart unity of self through my "odd-looking" dancing to this postural spectrum. Nietzsche said everyone must find one's disco. do the ordinary everyday, live as variously as possible, become mom

at the house party we all wondered what happened
to Soul2Soul what happened to back to life back to
reality being reality? and not defined by isolating it on
the basis to an a priori reality? before then we defined
reality as reality itself. this was the premise of Mom's
recovery song from heroin in the 80s. we were all down
for it at the BBQ in the garden when art governed
our drives where campari was served alongside kush:
the consuming farrago of the times. Vegas was our
vernacular and go-go boys our choir as flesh resisted
the grim variegation of tainted platelets. white blood
cells counted the no. of sexual proclivities of the walls
and pavement in Repulsion: everything a threat to
virginity. Deneuve denuded

on cue hell's disco ball-drops like Róisín Murphy's Law.
we were prejaculatory. i wanted something: to live and
to live right now. a better sickle cell sac reaping. out at
sea outer space of luxury with a daddy maybe this is
the wrong song to feel estranged from wife-wanting. I
want the sound. i want the image over object. i'm told
the zest of life is a hunk on the dance floor pregnant
with futurity

speaking of movements: let's talk about this body-double 90s movie. convulsion of the body convulsion of the soul causing the I to autre. the director palmed a diagram of cause and effect the 2D'd woman Muybridging locomotion. material events fall away. what allows aesthetics to cohere in video are no longer in Vogue. every woman's body exists in relation to dad. freaks criminalize adult flirting and pop songs schematize this cliche. the computer i'm watching this film on moves itself into voiceover mode: *i don't know what i is* my headcase manager writes it's more productive to think of all the ppl who've already inhabited this gay. ah the fine art of hiding inside other people's minds. i read that somewhere about K Stew. that old sclerotic embrace of a film's pubic count and/or a celebrity's identity kiss. the quote originality end quote of copying another's hand-job, e.g. copyright's twilight zone. there's an app for that that's v apropos. *but do gays still exist?* asks the last one who died recently of boredom thru a cadaverous effect. while emphasizing the citation a booty shorts hug went longing. consider this the thrilling sum of you

MULHOLLAND RIVE

off-road in Dirt Mulholland in hollywood bedlam
death's pretty jaws riven action: the strangled american
actress gets covered by aussie cherries, splits skins.
shattering her unhappy mollusk, feet dabbing the
alabaster chips red. blurred filtering to a crazy haircut
that clearly knows what it's doing. they dyed and
switched bushes at across her ego estate. razor blade
clicks, blonded blended slipping innards into silencio.
some woman in this live film takes the bait. the bait
is the bartender in the other scene waking up to bad
cream. heaven is a sublingual armpit. endangered
fingertips tearing butterflies into bits of. when does
one just think i receive? i get stuffed to remember when
without complaint. Dad's spermoderm muffs airborne.
the poet disappears. i feel a trigger: the camera vomits
out of me

i step out of Elysium park, out of Elysian. my ideology our ideals change the ideal present ideology of new entertainments and new attainments. the training wheels broke as the highway fell in front of my doorway. deer-struck. my time vessel says it's 2 am: time to pull cars from wrecks. all these all black all brunette strands of hair had taken bleach in california. one conclusion is my Italian doctor, pills

if we need help when we jump into the swimming pool. my mom always said we thought they did. hm

MD MDMA Mollycoddled

my roommate from ontario (?) dipped peroxide. that pig needed a pen. need to un-meat. needed to draw cum over my face to feel good in her pretty pink sty

a plot constructed around the theft of someone's "personality"

this was conceived before the film was completed but after production had begun. the two leads murdered out back. two images to sieve through fractals. but the woman has a 2D body she can't possibly. her overreaction doesn't bruise

mom says when a hen dies it can be auctioned off. the proceeds sent to a rescued organ

some things get better with burial says (The Director)

the canyon stopped crawling. amnesia is this brunette actress wearing a marbled blonde wig sandwich. an identifiable aroma of decay, predeceased

everything we see on this screen is an object fiction the killer eats us out: the chalk line separating the knife i left behind the birthday card from Mr. T the bad 80s clothing the previous day a game called *Bonkers*

all this drama? me. i'm the Clown, i'm the priestess. i'm the way the hardwood inhales its dust the way the spider in the corner looks like shit leaking darkroom chemicals

yet i somehow worked a garment at the beginning of the story, squeezed my little fox. developed a nightmare about a $90 West Elm Street crystal. i'm told eating a broad bean is Latin for *dumb*. meanwhile the powder machine keeps accusing me of being homosexual keeps barfing nurses at me keeps accusing me of having a beautiful oedipal complex later at the party the headless server tells me people who provide online with pictures are the backbone. a guided mediation on extinction. in the kitchen pesto got pounded, the clown semen soured. i reach out to touch the fake swimming pool keep getting jammed trying to thread a garden hose through an antique keyhole. thread her tender data through the POV: the old VHS tape being choked to spool

blood is a terrific thing to use says the son of a plastic surgeon. the toothpick sticking an olive's violence is a pallet to my wife standing nude a shrine to my Catholic guilt complex

stripper heels neck snaps

suddenly my Birkin bag clutches huge knocking the cruel bitch of fate. across the way a monster lurks in a rented room behind a mirror as the dangling bulb bares its yellowed grime bares us naked up to the dusty surface of a pool raft toward an urge to merge with. hopeless dreams of being

sleep pools around our eyes now for a long time to

west of north hollywood is where Kim lives. also she's not Kim. nonetheless she enlightens us about a video on air-conditioner repair. (*i try not to hear that loud air conditioner in Encino*). turns out suicide is the same in every language. but in Calabasas i'll take this cowboy over the snakeman. when he shows me the cage with the 5-foot housewife i feel a twinge of jealousy and begin identifying as the muscle cars Lana del Rey sings about on the bedroom bear carpeting the intelligentsia the Castrati and the Emasculates are enjoying a Fiona Apple album called go grab a hammertoe or whatever. someone's talking about Carl Jung's lonely girl-on-girl archetype and that someone is me. we tend to synchronize with the other. tension is the baseline of this awful song and that's what makes suburbia bearable. mom says in the dresser i kept a sex diary and later got blamed for my own murder drugs avail themselves of their enclosures. i'm beached again. the doors jamb spiders. somebody wonders aloud *is Cameron Diaz flammable?* everyone in my house wears a bodybag. that fake handbag? she was me. she was lovely and nude, tanned and exhausted. she didn't care that he was sidled up next to her while she slept in her wet, brined

the morning after i couldn't remember the password to my typewriter, nor why my words went translated into phlegm. precariousness is a condition needed to learn anything, to wreak havoc on the hierarchy between voice and song. this old futon's stain was linked to the consumption of images. either way you are as hot as a word might spell. either way my dead-behind-the eyes look became fantasy island

so i became one of her, Middle Age, unfamous body
bag. i rolled my eyes out at their tales: some EMT found
our celebrity neighbor at the bottom of her stairs, a
head-to-foot hematoma. injuries were categorized and
tabloided. they told these spooky stories picnicking at
the food court mall, a cemetery where people ate on top
all the men in my family who died prematurely. the rest
disappeared into chambers so no stories about them.
outside Panda Express mom filled me in on cancer.
she said the doctors removed a necroctomy, part of an
abdomen not a neck, a colon slash cornea. *we're already
deaaaaaaaaaaad* she tarred onto me. i leaned forward
into my sticky chicken as a scattered alphabet hanged
itself across a menu. wiping my finger on a few inches
of napkin separating us the dead from the living.
outside everyone was in a coma, their bodies a shop to
go klepto on. inside the dark theater lies carpet touched
by human fingers. *We're barely here* mom says without
speaking. behind the glass windows was the ocean, the
tree, a beard, a button-up white collar, weird Venetian
masks. inside it was air-conditioned, weatherless

now i'm back in the latter, the 20th century: meat-soft
mouth, pink, garlic-full blood on stucco walls and water
jars painted with palmtrees, unisexual. Malibu. the
taste of melon, raw slithery-wet skin, your breath and
your kisses that kill. out of humility, i shave my hair,
watch others make love to you through me, a stream
of lovers. yes, a stream in the literal: one continuous
excretion, tears or blood of marking. i learn to be more
like Sade (the singer) who foiled and loved and had
it right. for all that i cannot be in matter, this is the
cracked glass where i might erase all my poorly written
histories. these Pacific shores, their skylight dawning.
bluegreen ever-slaying luminescent ocean, organisms
making light for one another's

ACKNOWLEDGEMENTS

No writer d(r)ives alone. Thanks to Kaitlyn, Leza, and Christoph. To my mother, of course. And to Anna, always.

ABOUT THE AUTHOR

Vanessa Roveto is the author of two books of poetry, *bodys* and *a women*, and the novella *The Valley (a void)*. She is the recipient of a MacDowell Fellowship. She lives in Los Angeles.

ALSO BY CLASH BOOKS

GENDER/FUCKING
Florence Ashley

REGRET OR SOMETHING MORE ANIMAL
Heather Bell

EARTH ANGEL
Madeline Cash

LA BELLE AJAR
Adrian Ernesto Cepeda

SEPARATION ANXIETY
Janice Lee

SAD SEXY CATHOLIC
Lauren Milici

WAR IS NOT MY MOTHER
Vi Khi Nao

THE SORROW FESTIVAL
Erin Slaughter

INTERNET GIRLFRIEND
Stephanie Valente